I would like to first thank trust, faith and belief in me. You gave me the time and resources to help me create something great, and I thank you. I owe everything to you, and I thank you for always being by my side, delivering your kindness and love through out some of my worst situations. You stood by me in this entire process, and I am appreciative of that. There will never be anyone that can replace you, and I dedicate this book to you! I love you with all my heart.

I would like to thank my grandparents, Henry & Bernice. Thank you for helping teach me to believe in myself. You two are not only loved, but also greatly appreciated.

I would like to thank my ex wife, Asia Pleasants. Though we are no longer together. It was you, who held me together, and gave me my backbone in many situations when I went astray. Thank you for all that you have contributed in my life. Especially for giving me my most prized gift, our son, Massiah Shannon. Whom, I love dearly with all my heart.

To my aunt, Tiffany, who helped steer me and teach me first hand on the things that take place within the urban community. I thank you! You were my eyes and my teacher throughout life. You built awareness in my journey and I will always be thankful for that.

Most importantly I would like to thank my cousin Stevie. Who in all actuality steered me straight and kept me head strong throughout a very pivotal time in my life. Thank you for always being one phone call away. Thank you for always giving a listening ear when needed, and helping me stay in the ring. When I wanted to throw in the towel. You were one of the first people who believed in my dreams, and told me to accomplish it. " For a man waits for nothing or no one. " You have been there through my darkest days, and for that you will always remain dear to me. I thank you for all that you have contributed within my transition into a man.

Thank you to all of my close friends and family. I thank all of you for helping contribute to my success and growth, and always being there for me as well.

I would like to thank you, the reader, for taking the time out to read this body of work. Whoever you may be, just know I created this from the love of my heart. With the certainty and mission to change our communities and our society, and your concern to read such material goes to show that you have the ability and concern to do the same. Let's help raise the bar, because the life we influence may not just be our own!

Thank You,
Jerard Shannon

FOREWORD

Thank you for taking out the time to purchase this book. If I told you I created this without the inspiration of so many other authors I would be lying. The "Memoirs of a modern day slave" has been created with the use of outlooks that were dependent on the stories of so many great autobiographies. Those of in which include the narrative story of Fredrick Douglas, The autobiography of Malcolm X, and most importantly Succeeding against the odds The Autobiography of a Great American Businessman. These three helped mold and create my own personal outlook on society.

With great pleasure I present to you my views, and my beliefs. I will hope that this book helps open

the mind of the reader to become more involved in what surrounds him or her.

My purpose is to inform, teach, and educate. I have set forth in doing so by completing this book so I can solely do just that. Educate! The problems we face as blacks within society have been overlooked. However, it's time to place our main focus in what has gone unattended. No government or politician can see to that.

The Memoirs of a modern day slave represent the plights blacks face today in modern society. It represents the struggle to live a life of comfort and acceptance. What is being seen on our television screens is not what's being in our communities. The days of physical slavery may be behind us, but the days of mental slavery are not. We are locked into a system that does not shackle us with chains on our wrists and ankles, but instead on our minds.The option to break from this slave mentality is for you as the reader to take into consideration. I ask that you remove the shackles from your brain, and free your mind!

CONTENTS

Short Stories

High Rise for Low Standards

Is it the Shoes?

Prepackaged

And where do most dreams end up?

DEAR BLACK AMERICA

Today I promised my momma her baby boy wouldn't return without the world. Thereafter, I walked outside onto the plantation. I witnessed the usual daily activity that we have succumbed to. Master (police) overseeing his slaves, every bit of the way as they work his corners, and traffic his drugs. I view him promising our entrepreneurs (hustlers) their independence all while he keeps them mentally imprisoned .I then shift my attention not to far from my fellow business men, and begin to focus on a moving group of my beautiful sisters; who I suspect to be currently nursing and care taking masters babies. Babies who will soon be raised to work master's plantation; replacing the same existing slaves who stand right before them. Their unconditioned minds which will soon be influenced by our culture. A culture that is filled with violence, exploitation, and the consumption of materialistic possessions. They too will dream big and then tricked by this countries reality.

During my observation I was interrupted by a call. To my astonishment this phone call, challenged my pride. It challenged my dignity. It challenged my history, and most importantly it challenged my intelligence. This call demanded a decision, and that decision demanded an answer. I had to decide whether to continue to follow the millions of people who have become mentally enslaved or to go to war. My decision then was made. I hung up the phone, and not to long after. I enlisted myself to go to war.

Young black America, we have been losing at this war. The

media has tricked us that we have won this battle some years ago. That our ancestors who have fought and risked their lives, have now overcome there feet's and are now victorious and triumphant. However I am here to tell you that we have not!

No longer will I*, be tricked by society and it's tactics. No longer will I*, settle for what our government considers politically correct. No longer will I* believe what the media tells me.

I know you care to not join me against our fight on the frontier. But for the few that do. I ask that you load your gun. You don't have a gun you say? No worries my fellow friend. The gun I speak of is your mind. Load your mind with knowledge, power, and truth. Become informed and educated. This war is to be fought using mental strength, not physical.

Today, I step foot onto the battlefield. I will be going to war for you! To show that we are more then what meets the eye. I will prove that we are smarter then what society believes. I will go on to break the barriers that still exist. Please wish me the best. "I LIVE for you. I'll DIE for you! "

*The stars represented in the letter, are for my own personal feelings and beliefs. Not to be forced onto anyone.

THE RISE OF A PEOPLE

The red or the blue pill? The "red" pill is a symbol, a symbol of my desire to return to reality. With the selection of the red pill, my destiny has been chosen. You should know that fate would play apart of my life much sooner than later. It would only become a matter of time, before I would accept it.

On May 3rd, I was cloaked in my African academic regalia. On this day, I received my Bachelors of Science Degree in front of an audience of a much rather large group of people. Not only people, but "my people." The feeling was glorious. Soon there after, I was welcomed into the very place I have been sheltered from. The real world! This is the beginning of my arrival.

Often I am reminded that action builds character. Though I am often faced with the departure of the place that nurtured me as a young man. I am always reminded of the open arms I was greeted with upon my return. For now, I must train and become prepared for the very thing my institution has prepared me for. The ability to fight and remain strong through what some may call hard times. I was taught to use mind over matter, remain stern, and never give up. I thank my alma mater, Johnson C. Smith University! So here we go.....

After the 'red pill' was consumed. I admittedly took notice to my community and the segregation that still exists; along with the gentrification happening in out country. I was told that this might be a "tough pill to swallow ", and once swallowed. I nearly CHOKED!

Always given the opportunity to linger amongst the presence of others. The "street scholars" took me in. Many of who have lived my day, years ago. With their authorization, they entrust their knowledge and power in me. On NOVEMBER 21ST, 2010, MY DESTINY UNFOLDED IN FRONT OF MY EYES. The moon shined bright, the stars aligned, and my GOD GIVEN GIFT WAS AWAKENED. I never fell in love with time, as much as I did on that day. So many questions unraveled, and supplied with answers. I began peaking with the linguistics of Cassius Clay, using the wisdom of Cornell West, and the delivery of JAY-However not quit as sharp as Malcolm X! I have been offered the lessons.

My world since then has not been the same. For years I have seen and watched the pain of the urban community, but never have I heard the cries. I can now understand why the world is not ready for "OUR" story.

With the resource of education and literature, I will shine the light on what you left to grow in the dark. Watch as your unattended seeds grow and blossom, from the light. These words are the water that I will use daily to watch my people sprout.

INTRUSION OF THE AMERICAN DREAM

Excuse my intrusion. The people that you see on the right of me are here to receive what they deserve. Yes, we are here to infiltrate your American Dream. Your inception has just been intercepted by the very least of your worries. For centuries you slept comfortably. We have watched you enjoy the fruits of our labor; all while serving you with a smile. To your disbelief, that smile held an ulterior motive.

These motives have positioned us for this very day. It's taken almost 150 years for this day Several of our most important activist and leaders have lost their lives for this day, but the movement has moved on.

You tried very hard to erase our history and our culture. Needless to say we are innovators. You gave us peanuts. We gave you peanut butter. We are the creators of the very first civilization. My ancestors dedicated their lives to service you. All while planning for our return

I am the awoken one. With very little money, but much bigger pride. I provide my generation with today's modern day hope. Just like my older brothers, who opened the doors for me to enter your "American Dream". I aspire to give inspiration. This inspiration that will awaken many more like me. I dictate to them to use our brothers Malcolm X and Martin Luther Kings philosophies. First use mind over matter, but force BY ANY MEANS NECESSARY. I embed in them to use their mind first, and everything else second. To always use judgment but only against the likes of those who are deceiving.

It's only fair that I inform you that the culture that you have taken away from us, has been reconstructed. You over looked the Negro hymns we sung while working on your plantations. Which soon evolved into Hip Hop. The very thing you fear entering your household, without your consent, but still manage to penetrate the minds of these children. Giving us the ability to create multi million dollar entertainers who manage to give inspiration to people across the world.

You overlooked our physical strength, which soon over took sports once we was given the chance to "play". You overlooked our cooks, feeding us as cheaply as possible, often with throwaway foods on the plantation, forcing slaves to make nothing into something. We turned collards, ham hocks,, and corn meal into SOUL FOOD.

Most importantly you overlooked the many people who wanted to learn. You overlooked those who took the time to read, and decipher the very words you created (English). You overlooked those that took "a inch to get a yard" (Frederick Douglass). Who then in return wrote messages on loose-leaf paper, that would sustain the hands of time long enough to reach and inspire us.

Who once taught how to read, write, and type on your computers and mobile devices. Would then use your technology to get their messages out to millions.

This is the intrusion of your American Dream. The people you see on the right of me are here to receive what they deserve.

PERSEVERANCE

There was once a point in time when African Americans use to chant and root loudly for our heroes. Heroes like Joe Louis and Mohammed Ali. These men were praised by African Americas throughout the country. They were not only respected because of defeating their opponent but for defeating adversity as well. An accomplishment that created pride in who we are as a people.

In today's modern society, those loud chants, have been muffled and silenced, and people have since then forgotten about the hometown hero. The requirement of a fast dollar has eluded the equilibrium of the Afro- American, and has sense discontinued his or her sense of self-pride and ethics. Today's logic only revolves around the sense of social class and where you stand within it.

Social acceptance has been fought for because the image of "particular" people making it, has been satisfying. The mere thought of knowing that the American dream, is attainable with hard work has created the idea that activism is no longer needed. To have that ideology is wrong to say the very least.

There are still barriers being placed. Therefore making hurdles for us to jump over. We need to obtain things as a whole. Just one man or woman living a particular lifestyle is not feasible. The sight of seeing a African American president being elected is not enough to inspire hope, and faith in everyone. The call for extensive education, self-awareness, and career opportunities should flourish as well.

If you settle for less, you will only get less. We have a past with struggle, and fights, that have helped open the door of opportunity. However that door of opportunity requires you to be on the "guest list" in order to enter, There are not enough people protesting about the inequality that still remains relevant in the United States, not only for African Americans, but all minorities.

Often we hear a great deal of the "glass ceiling", but its about time that we break through the glass ceiling. To break through the glass ceiling, we must act as a unit. If we all form together as one, then things can be handled accordingly. All we need is will power.

We need the importance of, ethics, to be installed in us all. Ethics strengthens a person to fight for what they believe in. It creates morale and values. Ethics will help determine our level of prestige in society. Nothing without a fight can be won. Blacks as people will be seen and thought out to be a lower class, because of the state-of-mind we portray.

The time has come for us to become militant. To fight for what we want and need within our communities. A contribution needs to be made by all of us. To not only follow in what we see or what is given to us within the community. Comfort does not only lie within the mind, comfort lies within your home and community as well.

There has to be a fight willing to be put up by more then one individual. If we want to hear the chants we once heard when we overcame adversity. We must fight for what is being requested. Triumph and victory is only given to those who fight for what they believe in.

THE NEED TO FIGHT

I find that often we do not tend to fight for what we believe in. As the saying goes " If you don't stand for something, you will fall for anything." The thought of being submissive and not being in control of my own autonomy has always been disturbing to me. In life you have to fight for what you want, and for what you believe in.

Making wrong decisions in your past can most certainly haunt your future. A lesson that I had taught myself after a mistake I made during the summer of 2005. It was my first summer back home after my college break, in New Jersey, and I decided to attend West Indian carnival that took place in my hometown's downtown area. Fairly new to drinking, my friends and me decided to purchase a bottle of liquor, which in return would have affected a substantial amount of time in my life.

After the festivities had come to an end, we remained downtown to converse with a few females. Shortly thereafter the police, who proclaimed there was a man reported in a red shirt with a pistol. The police officers approached on of my friends, and begin to search him. During the time, I was inebriated and I decided to heckle the police officer and dispute the fact that the two officers chose to select us as the perpetrators due to our nationality. Needless to say, I found myself in a scuffle and then behind bars.

I went to trial for about a year, and received several charges. Charges in which were then placed onto my record. These charges led me to not becoming eligible to receive an occupation after my graduation from college. I had little to no idea that the small situation that I faced with police officers would affect my sustainability to obtain a job in my near future. If I had, I would have never made that attempt to justify something so petty.

After graduation, I looked high and low for a place of employment. Close to nearly no one would give me an opportunity due to the misdemeanor I had attained. It made me very depressed. Having the education and work skills to work for the places I applied for began to become very stressful. The stress added to my level of thinking, which certainly added to my level of sickness. There were days where I could hardly stand on both of my feet or eat for that matter.

After months of denial my dear aunt, who I still thank to this day, had given me a call about an opportunity to expunge my record. I have heard about the opportunity in the past but I knew that it had cost an expensive fee for a lawyer to do. However on the night of my aunts call. I was told it was being done for free. I took no time to put my clothes on and make my way to the Jersey City Public library to find out more information in hopefully having my record expunged.

When finally arriving, I was greeted by a group of individuals who all came to have their record expunged. We all waited excitingly to meet the person who was going to take the time out their schedule to help us expunge our records for free. While waiting we were given food, and a set of short papers to read. We all began to socialize and share the possible employment opportunities that awaited us after our record expungement.

After at least a hour and a half of waiting, we were all introduced by the man who created the program and was told that the person who was conducting the expungement would not be able to make it tonight, but be sure to come back next Tuesday night to receive his assistance. Everyone was very humble and all agreed to meet up the following week to do the same.

Next week came, and we all met back up again, like the last time we were all given files of papers on expungement and waited an substantial amount of time only to not be welcome by the person conducting the expungements again. Once again we were told to come back, and look forward to this person. I returned the following week and was given the same speech, only to give up hope, and never to return again.

While leaving, I finally took the time to look over the expungement papers that were given to me, and began to see that the papers taught the reader to do the expungement "themselves." I began to grow amazed and after three weeks of wasted time, I instantly began to work on the paperwork myself. I read the expungement papers day into night, and night into day, and began to create a rough draft. The process consisted of a lot time, but with my determination and focus I knew I could complete the expungement.

At the time I was on welfare, and if you were receiving welfare certain fees were waived, and you weren't subjected to pay. I saved over a thousand dollars doing my expungement, all with the thought, determination, and will power to erase a mistake I committed in the past. It wasn't easy, but I could no longer live with that mistake. In May, I was awarded a letter from the government, and CIA about the removal of my misdemeanor from my record. It took nearly three months for me to accomplish the goal, but I set it within myself to stand for something, and not fall for anything.

The only person that can stand for something in life is you. Nothing is given freely. I thank my grandmother for instilling in me the idea of never believing in the vocabulary term "cant." I thank my mother for raising me to always believe in myself, and instilling in me a sense of pride. I thank my university, that gave me an education, and allowed me to push myself to obtain an degree, because with knowledge comes power. It's important to believe in yourself and your capabilities.

Having been inspired by John H. Johnson (creator of Ebony and Jet magazine) Succeeding Against the Odds, The autobiography of a great American businessman, I now know the importance of taking a risk. A line said by John H. Johnson, from the book that was pivotal and detrimental to my own life " Failure is a word, I don't accept."

HISTORICALLY BLACK

"You all are stupid. I can't wait to go to college." I'll never forget that quote which came from a neighborhood friend during the year and time I was scheduled to graduate from high school. At the time I wasn't ashamed, nor was I amused with the thought of stepping foot on a college campus. I haven't even known anyone that went to college, so the thought was never occurred to me to further my education.

I also can't forget the nagging my aunt would do to my mother about my possible decision of not got going to decision. " Theresa if you don't send that boy to college, he's is going to grow up to be unsuccessful." Truthfully I just wanted to work at the United States Postal Service or be a drug kingpin like Tony Montana in Scarface. From time to time, my mother would try to influence me to go, but I still wasn't convinced. Until, finally she urged that I take the SAT. I decided to take the test and though I score very high. I maintained a decent score.

When it was time for me to decide on a college to attend. I decided to go against the grain, because in my heart I wanted to stay connect to what I knew. So I applied for all black colleges. When my aunt got word of this. She opposed and notified my mother to not allow me to make that decision. She stated that I would know become diversified, and I would not expand my horizons. My mother chose not to influence my decision. She was just happy that I finally made the decision to at least attend college.

When making the decision where to attend college, demographics and family, played a huge role in my ultimatum. So I made the choice of going to a small historically black university in Charlotte, N.C. It wasn't necessarily the university itself that captured my attention. I actually had family, who at the time, I thought would look after me and keep me in their best interest.

In the beginning of my attendance at the university I would just consider myself a young degenerate from the ghetto of Jersey City, New Jersey. Initially my intentions was to party, and sell whatever I could get my hands on because at that time. That is what I seen my father and people in my neighborhood do to survive. I only knew what I had saw growing up as a child. So I figured I would carry that way of life to the institution.

The first three years, while being there I didn't do much beside party; until I got into a fight with a group of guys. That fight helped change my direction and gave me the opportunity to move from my dorm. Down to a much smaller private residence section of the university where the more "serious" students took heed to their academics.

Once there, I met a lot of people who helped open my mind to the importance of education. I have to thank my father for taking the time to talk to persuading the residence counselor to relocate me. If my father didn't talk to the counselor, I do don't believe I would have completed college. At the time I didn't even have the grade point average to even step foot through those doors, but the residence counselor gave me a chance. It's amazing how someone beliefs can help you on your way to achievement.

When I finally moved in, I met great people and made great friends who helped me become the person I am today . I must admit when I moved in I was arrogant and ignorant. A deadly combination at the least, but with time I grew to become a much better man. I still struggled with my grades in the beginning until one of my roommates in the residency advised me that I get my grade point average together in order to be successful. At the time it didn't register with me. However, he explained it to me about how the real world works, and my place in it. A conversation I would never forget as well.

After that conversation, I was set out to accomplish and do as much as possible. I wanted the world and everything in it, and I seen in order to obtain those things. My fantasies of being a hustler or drug king pin like Scarface wasn't the way to acquire it. It took for me to sit and focus and use my mind over all things in order to achieve greatness.

There at that university I was taught the importance of finances, self-empowerment, and black culture. I was given opportunities I'm sure I would not have received being at a predominantly white institution. Everything was there for my taking, and I met wonderful seen my potential and believed in me. There was no competition between me and anyone else. We all stood together as a whole.

I must thank my aunt who encouraged that I furthered my education. Without her persistence, I don't know where I would be. Even though I must call bluff as, because though I wasn't surrounded by a large group of diversity. I was taught how to carry myself with pride, grace, and honor. Which is all due to a small historically black university.

THE GLOBAL EDUCATION INITIATIVE

It was November 20th, 2008 and the newly appointed dean of Johnson C. Smith, Dr. Ronald Carter, had launched his global education initiative. A initiative that allowed all of the universities students to receive a passport, without any expense. His vision was to have attending student's travel abroad to experience other cultures and languages. Once hearing about the opportunity I wasted no time, in acquiring my very own.

Many nights, I watched the foreign film, City of God, amazed by the beautiful scenery of a place vastly known for its beauty in landscape, women and culture. All with hopes and dreams to go there and see the place with my very own two eyes. It was the first time I watched a documentation and film of a lifestyle and culture that was relatable to the very one I grew up around. The only difference was the location, that being Rio de Jenario, Brazil.

Without little time wasted, I seen to Dr. Carter's initiative and began to pursue my thoughts of travel. I excitedly ironed my slacks along with my white collared shirt, and proceeded to put on a tie. When exiting my residency hall. I was asked what event was I dressed for, and evoked the minds of several people of the great opportunity I was preparing myself for. Many had thought me dressing up for a passport photo was ridiculous, but I simply did not see myself wearing a crew neck shirt while conducting business.

Upon my arrival at the room where the process for the passports was taken place at, I was given an application and number to wait to be called for my photo. To my surprise there was very little students in the room who took advantage of receiving their passport. All in which I found very shocking. I submitted my photo and information, and left there after only envisioning my dream to one-day visit the Rio de Jenario, Brazil.

Finally after three years of envisioning myself in Brazil, I embarked on my journey with my cousin Michael. Michael, like the dean of my alma mater, believes in the thought of traveling and seeing different places and cultures. A foreigner to the lifestyle of visiting different countries, he is not. Always looking for a new mission to embark on. He helped me with my journey toward my dream. Having had left several days before my arrival, I was to arrive there in Rio on my own. My first time out the country, and I traveled not knowing what to expect.

When I finally arriving in Rio, I was stunned by its beautiful beaches, and respect of the people in the small community and the easygoing lifestyle. No one seemed to focus on the hardships or concerns that we as Americans did, and social class and segregation wasn't enforced. While there I felt apart of the festivities that took place in the city.

One thing that sent me in disarray was the sight of its level of poverty. I witnessed families sleeping in the street next to establishments, all with comfort and ease. Families in which was the same race of my own. I seen people of color digging out the trash, and collecting cans off of the streets to possibly make money, and feed themselves the next day. I saw that the living standards of the ghettos are just as similar of those in the ghettos of America. Having seen the ripple effect of poverty internationally, made me fortunate of my own living standards. It made me want to improve the way of living for not only myself, but for those living in the states too.

I must admit everyone if giving the opportunity should do traveling abroad. I look forward to seeing more places, and building a better understanding for cultures. I had the opportunity to make friends with people from different parts of the globe while there.

If not given the opportunity to watch foreign films and obtain my passport from my university. I would have remain naïve and complacent with not wanting to visit the place of my dreams. It truly helped change my life and my outlook on what should and should not be taking seriously. The effects of having traveled internationally will always be detrimental to my approach and attempt at life.

ONCE UPON A TIME IN EGYPT

History always captured my attention as a child when I was younger. I was always fascinated by the accomplishments of others. The non-fictional facts of men and women overcome obstacles in the past. Nothing stood out to me more than the history of Ancient Egypt. The sight of pyramids, hieroglyphics, and tombs fascinated me. The pictures alone, spoke volumes to me and I was immediately drawn to that specific point of time in history.

While in college, I took a course on World Civilization. The professor was a very wise man that actually traveled the world and was very cultured. We were in-between the middle of the semester and was preparing to go into the next chapter of our history book, this chapter happened to discuss Ancient Egypt. The professor told us that for this chapter we would not learn from the book, but from visuals on a projector. This was very interesting and he managed to gain my attention immediately. I can't actually say that my eyes were prepared for what it was about to see over the course of the next week.

I remember vividly and soundly what I saw and what I heard from this professor. The images projected on that white board of Black Hieroglyphics and a *white man* telling and an entire class full of black students that this history belongs to US was astonishing. Here lied images of people that look exactly like us which was actually left thousand of years ago. Here was not only myself but also millions of other peoples history being displayed having had been hidden from them. On television and in history books lies run ramped, and the only thing taught within the school system is that the beginning of African American's history begins with slavery and the fight for equal opportunity and civil rights. I felt instant gratification when I seen these images. I didn't know to jump for joy or become angry. Though I felt a sense of relief, I was disappointed with the fact that I had no knowledge of my *real* history.

Needless to say that after that course ended, things would never be the same for me. I grew a much larger infatuation for Egyptian History. After graduating college ,I went to see the King Tut Exhibit at the Discovery Museum in New York City. I purchased tickets without a thought in mind, and waited patiently for the day to arrive.

The day had finally come, and I made my way through New York City to finally see the history and images that my professor displayed from his projector. While there the first thing I immediately noticed was the fact that there was not one single Afro American in sight. It solidified the fact that it wasn't Afro Americans didn't want to engage in seeing their history. But I believe that is because their history wasn't being *taught* to them. As we began the tour, the museum showed a short film clip, which would depict King Tut during his day of rule. The TV. Once again displayed white actors whisking through the desert and sitting on thrones. I looked on in disbelief and disgust with the lies that were continuously projected.

After the film was over, the doors opened up to the exhibit and we were allowed in. Inside the truth was revealed. The images on the screen decimated from my mind, and I was presented with the artifacts that were left behind by the people who truly lived the lives, that film producers and directors wrongfully depict. Here I witnessed small and large statues of Nubian men and woman. These images of Pharaohs and Queens who bear the sight of having thick wooly hair. I could not believe the audacity of the people who created the short film!

I began to seek more information about the Pharaohs and Queens who once walked this earth, and begin to draw comparisons to those people I walk amongst each day . These people did not die and disappear from the face of the earth. Their bloodline still exists. We just cannot draw exact correlation to their existence, but the way of thinking and movement is here living within us.

After my visit to the King Tut exhibit I was determined to visit Egypt to see the truth! For my 25th birthday, I decided to book a trip to Egypt. Initially I had high hopes of going to Luxor to visit the Valley of the Kings, but the timing would not permit for it . A lot of people were amazed by my decision. Especially with Egypt recently going through a revolution, and the people of the city seeking liberation. Also the leader of Libya, General Gadhafi, had just recently been captured and killed by the rebels who also wished for liberation and democracy. Logically it wasn't the best time to travel to North Africa but to me it was wise to do so financially while the Egyptian economy was down.

The day had finally come, and I found myself boarding a 13-hour flight to Egypt. I was afraid and excited. Once I arrived, I immediately noticed a change in environment. The people were inviting and friendly opposed to those in America. I booked my own driver and tour guide before I arrived, and was greeted by driver at the airport. He welcomed me with a warm greeting, and considered me his brother. I was actually surprised that he wasn't surprise that he would be escorting a young black man. After picking up my luggage and going through customs I met my tour guide and driver for that specific day, Bishon and Soloman. They were very polite and we began to have conversations about the economy, politics, and housing market. I must honestly admit that I truly felt at home and all the fear and doubts went away.

After checking in my hotel, I took the opportunity to

explore around, and noticed everyone treated me differently. I wasn't sure if it was the fact that I was young, alone, and boarding at a 5 star hotel or if it was because of the complexion of my skin. The people there greeted me in such a way, that I felt like royalty.

The following day I began my tour and was accompanied by my main tour guide and driver Mahmoud and Mohammad. Two very young Egyptians, who by the end of the trip did not just become my friends, but my brothers. These two men took me in and didn't treat me as the usual tourist. I really was looking forward to visiting the Pyramid of Giza and the Egyptian Museum. I visited Saakara and Memphis, all before returning back to Giza to see the pyramids. Once we finally arrived I was given the opportunity to climb the pyramid on my own, and take out a moment to myself to enjoy it. I sat on the pyramid and reflected on the past and what it may have felt like to be a pharaoh. It was like nothing I could have imagined or what I thought I knew or seen in a textbook .It was absolutely beautiful.

What detrimental part of my trip was the fact that, I was being asked what part of 'Africa" was I from? It truly hurt not being able to answer that question people due to the fact of slavery, which caused not only myself but also millions of other Afro- Americans to be unaware of their heritage. Being outside of America you actually have the opportunity to see, understand, and feel the power of being Afro- American. While there in Egypt I wasn't seen as an uneducated and ignorant black man as America portrays the men of my ethnicity to be. I could walk the street with a sense of pride and acceptance.

Before my leave, I visited the most important part of my trip, the Egyptian museum. Before entering I was told to be sure to leave all cameras behind, because they were not permitted inside. I remember fondly being told the exact same thing at the exhibit in New York and I promised not to leave Egypt without being able to reveal the truth. Once inside, I was given a private tour of the tombs and hieroglyphics, and then given the grand tour of King Tut's casket and treasures. Everything inside his corridor was made of pure gold . It was amazing but what was even more shocking was to see more statuses and hieroglyphics of the "boy king" being displayed as a black man. He had statues that depicted those in his hierarchy that were black. His throne had a picture of him and his wife, which was black, two guardian statues before you entered his burial chamber that were also black!

. After the tour my tour guide gave me the opportunity to once again roam freely. With that time, I took every single picture on my camera phone as possible. I had to tell my story. I wanted the people that I knew to see and understand our history and the way I felt, and that could not happen without those photographs. I took the risk of being kicked out the museum and having my phone confiscated. Luckily I was fortunate enough to capture as many pictures as I could without being caught.The time came for my exit, and I had finally achieved a goal of mine. Before my departure I enjoyed a dinner cruise on the Nile River and my tour guide Bishon, purchased a cake for me to help celebrate my birthday. It was definitely the best experience I ever had in my entire life. I was welcomed to come back anytime, having had made great friends. I remember reading how Malcom X felt after traveling to and returning from Africa, and I believe I could actually relate. I must say the reception during my stay was extremely beautiful. The people in Egypt may be financially poor, but they have a wealthy spirit. Within the next few years underneath a new government and rule I'm sure society will return to normal.

PEACE BE UPON YOU

"Rise Again!" These are the unspoken words of a people. This is their pain and suffrage. I am here for enlightenment, and not to be politically correct. I am here to plant the seeds into the minds of a generation. I made a decision to remain ignorant when it comes down to the logistics of "English and Journalism." I view this as a talent, which helps showcase my natural gift, motivational speaking. So therefore I do not wish to seek perfection within something that is not my specialty.

Jay-z told his listeners on the track titled, The Prelude, off of the Kingdom Come album. "I'm a hustler, disguised as a rapper." Metaphorically speaking, I'm not an author. I sell Motivation. Writing is my outlet. Journalism is not mine to perfect. It is here to use to my advantage to showcase my love to those who are "forgotten." Helping me to build empowerment in the people within my diaspora."

With that being said I would like to apologize to my "Queens,". I would like to take a moment and express my sorrow on behalf of not only myself but for all the misguided and mislead pharaohs! I apologize for not standing by you, and expressing my emotions to you. I apologize even more that this has to be showcased in literature. When all it simply could have taken was a phone call .I do wish for you to know that you are worshiped and loved because you are symbol of "The cycle of LIFE." Everything has been taught and learned by you. I am very merciful to your existence. For these circumstances alone, you shall forever be held with recognition as a "goddess."

To the broken and misguided "queens" Allow me to bring to let you know that there are good men out here in the world. The media is depicting and slandering your Pharaohs to be conniving, malicious, and vindictive. These are false allegations. There are in this world that respect women down to their cuticles, but it is up to our women to invest their time and heart into them. There are pharaohs who are seeking true love and companionship. Not every pharaoh is after you for your physical appearance. There are people who wish to know you for you.

Queen, We (pharaohs) have lost our way. For we have been beaten and broken mentally. The meaning of life is not about independence. The meaning of life is about dependency. Depending on someone to share love with. In return it compensates you with nourishment! I ask that you put your faith and belief into our pharaohs, and watch a boy blossom into a man.

I ask. If love is free? Why did so many before us have to die for our independence? With the usage of Love. "WE" can REBUILD A EMPIRE!

AWAKENING OSIRIS

Sleepwalking is the only way I can come to terms of what I now view through my pupils. As I watch from a designated area. I begin to view the movements of a people whom are "great." I began to notice some characteristics that are displayed in each one of my brothers. No matter how short or tall, small or big. Each one of my brother's walks with their heads held high. An undeniable characteristic that cannot be taken away from these men,

When I first began writing this passage, my body was slumped. Immediately after typing the word undeniable characteristics of my people. My back slowly began to rise. The power of my ancestry began to focus its attention onto my posture. For I shall NOT be seen with my head hung low. It is not my place in the world to do so.

For years my people have been broken. Forced to believe they are not the "chosen" ones. For years they have been manipulated to believe they are inferior to other creeds of men. For centuries we have been forced to only contribute to the grunt work within society within the working class. Forced to believe our true position does not call upon us to take complete control of our very own existence

The days of fooling us are slowly coming to an end. There is a heavy demand, and this country is failing to deliver. Fortunately, the thieves of the world could not have stolen the most important "NATURAL" resource from the richest country on this planet? What is the most natural resource you ask? THE ORI-GINAL MAN from AFRICA, creator of all things possible. That's who!

We are the originators of style and fineness. Without us there would be no need for competition. The world has built it-self off of its approach to compete with the people of very little words, but much stronger character. Before shrines, sculptures and monuments. The original man was seen as a symbol. A sym-bol of "Godliness." Now, I ask that you do not take the context of "Godliness" from "God. We are a splitting image of our lord and our savior. God is divine. So if man is a splitting image of his cre-ator. Then how can we not be seen as impeccable? As I grow wiser, this question baffles me.

My observation has come to teach me, that though we are no longer "physically" enslaved we are now "mentally" enslaved. Yet, find that even though we may not know we are pharaohs, and people of a higher power. We still have the ability to put it on display, because no matter what other races may think of us. We still refuse to conform! It is not in our bloodline to follow. We are meant to be trendsetters, and follow what "we" consider to be right.

During my observation, I began to see the modern day pharaohs. With each one seen, I began to view an uncanny resem-blance in each one. I began to notice that most of them were wear-ing hats. I am suddenly reminded that the ancient pharaohs wore head garments to symbolize their position of power. My mind begins to race and I began to trace my finding back to our roots. As I visualize all of our great pharaohs who once walked and ruled this earth (Ramses the Great, King Tutankhamen, and Akhen-aten). I began to take notice that they were never seen without their "crown." The exact same way Afro American men are with their hats. It is our "modern" day crown. From east to west and north to south; this trend is everywhere. A clear indication that it is still within us to be greeted as PHARAOHS!

The traits and history is undeniable. The last pharaoh to be buried was on June 25th 2009. At the end of a decade, and the beginning of a new born society. The King of Pop, Michael Jackson, was laid to rest. My observations of him being a pharaoh within modern day times is simple. HE INFLUENCED THE WORLD AND WAS LAID TO REST IN A 14-karat GOLD CASKET! He was buried in the same grace and elegance of his ancestors. The same of his idol was buried, The Godfather of Soul, JAMES brown. Who also might I add was buried in a 14-karat GOLD CASKET! The history is undeniable. It is the bloodline of my people.

The continent, the resources, and our legacy have been taken away from us, but our mentality has not. If you think like a king, the world shall receive you as a king. If you think as a slave, the world will treat you as such. The world has forgotten that we as a people "Work like slaves, but live as kings." The power is within us, to remember and continue to do so. We are already walking in the image of royalty, but it is now time to begin living as royalty.

AWAKEN & RISE! For you know not what you do. Your power cannot be contested. You are a undeniable force. Once you place your mind what it is for you to become. I can only supply you with the words of advice to take initiative. The rest is up to you.

LET THE STORY BEGIN

I'm use to a collegiate surrounding. So, I'm encouraged to spark dialogue and provoke thought at any chance I'm given. A year ago I was placed under psychiatric treatment for my extraordinary gift. The "gift of gab." I find myself having premonitions I stand firm in my beliefs and I strongly understand that most people are not going to be able to relate to me. However, I try to relate to others. I would like to believe that I am a realist and a equality.

I believe America has learned from their mistake of not protecting great leaders from the urban communities such as Martin Luther King, Malcolm X, and Huey P. Newton. All three leaders had a mission to advocate for change. Not only for Afro-Americans, but all Americans. Society could not understand their contribution. However , their lives had an effect on the world.

I would like to also note the influence of one of my personal aspirations, Tupac Shakur. A man who vaguely used his pain, discomfort, and intellect as a aesthetic and grasped the attention of millions. Not only did he become one of Americas most beloved musicians, but he became an ICON.

Through many interviews from an early youth to his adulthood, you could literally see the multiple changes in both mood and behavior. I read one case study where the writer actually believed Tupac suffered from bipolar. An accusation I truly find possible when dealing with someone full of passion and vision.

People who do not share this energy cannot relate. They see these people as manic or full of mood swings but what do you expect from a person who mind races consistently due to the knowledge they have obtained. Reading actually elevates ones mind. Most professionals study only one subject. Unlike professionals, people who read various materials to develop a sense of different professions and subjects becoming a pantologist. It should be known that if one is a Pantologist and practices pantology there is no way this person could maintain only one ideology. You will constantly see the shift in behavior once these people learn and obtain knowledge.

I'd also like to draw comparison to the attachment from ones environment. No matter how far a person goes. There will always be a desire to remain true to the place they were raised

I being born and raised in a poverty stricken environment. Have not lost my urge or motivation to "Be the Change I would like to see." I believe a lot of people lost their cause and vision when it comes o impacting society.

I really want to leave a legacy before I die. I know its uneasy for most people to talk about death, but it comes as a easy subject to me. I see death as nothing more than the conclusion of a story. I'm more concerned with what I do before death than the actual thought of death. We all must die one day. That's one thing that is guaranteed in life. I believe you must do all that you can possibly do while alive.

With that kind of mentality, I guess you can see why a psychiatrist would diagnose a person with "delusions of grandeur". A man from the ghetto, who has the ambitions to obtain all that this world, has to offer.

I find it amazing how magazine publishers can print periodical journals, like the Robb Report, and Wall Street Journal. Readers of these publications would essentially develop an urge to possess the objects and lifestyle being projected. So, when asked about the reader's intent to obtain these outlandish items or lifestyle. Would he or she have delusions of grandeur?

I have traveled to over 4 countries and have been to places where people of a higher status have not been. I don't necessarily feel this places me above anyone in society. However, I do believe it makes me more socially aware than most. I have actually seen the artifacts of Pharaohs and Queen. Which has enabled me with the mindset of Kings & Conquers.

Society has convinced us that we as a people, let alone 1 person should not think at these levels. I denounce all people who pose an opposition to people who think like this simply for the fact that empires and entire nations have been built on the mind set that psychologist and psychiatrist considerably say I suffer from. It truly is astonishing that the mindset that I have is one of which still helps keep Queen Elizabeth and her entire lineage as one of the most recognizable royal families in today's modern world.

Society sophisticatedly eradicated and replaced gladiators, warriors, and kings and queens with the face of one driving force. It goes with no surprise as in to why corporations advertise their products and services with brands. It is due to dominance that is used to remind the general public who is in control. I ask "you be the judge." However, I do know this. There is a shift underway. A shift unaccepted by those in control, which is primarily the 1 percent. This change is happening fast and is uncontrollable.

A new culture, formed as a religion. It's a sonic wave and it's to late to change. As said by Erykah Badu, "Hip Hop is bigger than the government", and with it those people who have undermined it will be toppled. I attest most of my drive and achievements to music. Beginning from Michael Jackson to it's newly anointed orchestrator Kanye West. I wouldn't be or have done what I've done without them.

At this point it is not hard to also say that our beloved Nina Simone was clearly correct in her song titled "New Day". She was gifted enough to see the future, and she too was diagnosed with bi polar disorder. However, history cannot rewrite her out of the books, and what she has contributed to not only music but also society. This chapter is an ode to Miss Simone, and the future. From new movies such as Black Panther that has broken box office records, all the way to Jay Z and Beyoncé who are now being seen in the light of being a Royal Family. I say, "Let the story begin."

MOBILIZE, EDUCATE, AND INVEST

I would like to 1st start by saying "We must contribute in order to gain prosperity."

We want to be individuals instead of thinking collectively as a unit.

All other minorities here in America are gaining from the attributions made through & from Afro Americans. Which is truly sad. It's sad how we completely fell to the waist side. We're more so happy to work a job than to accumulate wealth.

How was W.I.C created by Panthers only to then have the concept stolen by the government? Have you questioned who are the majority of people gaining and reaping the benefits from the Panthers construction?

After I graduated college I could not find a job so I was on welfare for a brief amount of time. I noticed the mass majority of people who were collecting were Hispanics (along with Jews) and very little Afro Americans. They understand how to work "our" system. They put each other onto their inside strategy. Most of them understand the importance of working together in their community. They are not shameful of taking advantage, and do it with esteem and pride. Before you continue the article, I would like to go on record that I'm an Equalist, and I am in no shape or form a racist. I believe in *"equality for all mankind"*.

I along with the census understand that Hispanics are eventually going to run most of America through population. There is an underlying agenda. Whenever you fill out a job application have you ever noticed it asks if you are Caucasian or Latino first before they mention any other race? That alone should make you aware of what the future dictates. So as a people we must learn to adapt.

What troubles me is when Donald Trump 1st began to campaign. He initially spoke about the immigration troubles we have as a country, and border control. Hispanics spoke up but who really came running to their defense? Black people. We began going to his campaign rallies as "Black Lives Matter Protesters", which created a distraction from the underlying message. We aimed with a cause but missed the target. Why do we have to be the 1st group of individuals to rise to the occasion and defend everyone else except our own?

We need to first unify as a people, and then mobilize. We have a voice but to many opinions. We require guidance and leadership. Us voting in the 1st Black President was a great accomplishment. However, it still did not contribute to our improvement. Was him being elected into presidency aspirational? Yes. Will he have a legacy that will solidify him within history? Yes. Will any of his policies help towards the Afro American community? No! We overlooked the need of not just only having the recognition, and representation of a Black President. But the need of an actual plan, strategy, and initiative that should come along with being in the oval office.

Unfortunately this can be told to Afro Americans repetitiously and they still will not understand. They won't understand why or how they are struggling even when you give them the answer, because it's to complex to comprehend. When in reality, it's truly not. Which is why we will move on to the importance of investing as a community.

The Afro American community has a trillion dollar buying power. However, we don't contribute or own anything within our community. Our communities are all owned and operated by everyone else except the people who live there. Chinese restaurants owned by Asians. Liquor stores owned by Indians. Pizzerias owned by the Italians. Grocery markets and bodegas owned by Hispanics. Chicken shacks operated by Arabs. What are the majorities of places we own? Barber shops, Beauty salons, and peddlers license used to sell merchandise from a small table on the very streets we own nothing on. We promote entrepreneurial-ship; but let's think about entrepreneurial-ship within our community without the inability of having investors.

When you contribute to an entrepreneur or business owner, if you will, (within the black community). The money goes into the owner of the business and not back into the community. Now it's not to say the owner does not want to contribute back to his community. We have to look at the reason why the owner is unable to invest back into his community. It's because once he gets a sell. That money is split into 3 ways. It must be reinvested into inventory, overhead, and personal expenses the owner has.

Now, let's discuss the importance of investing opposed to entrepreneurial-ship. When you invest in a company. You're guaranteed to see a return on your investment. The return may not be as big as you're expecting. However, once you began to invest you will then become a shareholder of that business or corporation you invested in. Now what would happen if "WE" began to invest into corporations as a whole or community? Well it's simple. Once we are unified, and mobilized then we will be able to attend shareholder meetings. Then we will be able to dictate to the corporations that we have invested in. Which will then change the playing field because with "our" voice. We can demand to open their door to us and bring jobs and businesses back into our community. Yes, 1 person could do it individually, but together as a unit. The demand becomes greater.

"We don't need just the crumbs from the table. We need a seat at the table, and a slice of the pie."

You ever wonder why the jobs are going overseas? Well it is because other countries understand the power of investing into businesses, infrastructure, and land. If they become the majority of shareholders the corporations have no choice but to adhere to them .You can begin to research this by looking into "**Sovereign Wealth Funds**". It's bigger than just bringing jobs and opportunity overseas for cheap labor and expenses! There is power in numbers. Have you asked why Indians operate most Dunkin Donuts or Subways? Well, its because they invested into these franchises and capitalized. Have you asked why foreigners are buying up the majority of real estate in New York?

"The days of wanting to obtain and live the American Dream are over. We are going into a global economy. We have to now think internationally and on a global scale."

We know nothing about the stock market or investing within the black community and what is known. Is rarely shared or discussed. Very little people understand the power behind it . We need financial advisors who are willing to teach financial literacy in our community. The importance of investing and becoming shareholders of what we buy and not only being proud paying consumers. We must begin to buy into our communities and stop selling out. If we take and apply the same format these countries are doing amongst each other with the, Sovereign Wealth Funds, we WILL flourish.

Gentrification is contributing to our demise. It will help eradicate us from not only what small amount we have but where we stay. Where are we all going to go once there is no place for us to migrate? Who is going to sell us back our homes; once the land is taken from right beneath us. Who will come to our aid? Personal feelings, attitudes, and lifestyles must now be put to the side. We must no longer be selfish, but selfless. We must contribute towards a purpose. Not for us, but for our children's children. So they will be protected and righteously looked after. The only way we can guarantee that is by investing and putting our buying power towards a cause.

OWN BOSS

"Own boss, own your masters, Slaves, The mentality I carry with me to this very day. Fuck rich, let's get wealthy, who else gon' feed we?"-*Jay-z*

I remember most song lyrics very vaguely, but this is one specific song lyric I will never forget by musical artist Jay-z. That line has not only brought wisdom to me, but it also has helped spawn and inspire my very need to obtain ownership in any and everything I pour my hard labor into. Slaves were not taught the importance of ownership. So as a result, very few of their offspring were taught the importance of ownership, wealth, and finances.

My mother always would recite a well-known quote known in the urban community to me, which was, "Always save for a rainy day." As an adolescent, I never knew what that quit meant, but it did instill in me, the urgency to always keep a few dollars around. While growing up, I rarely needed money going on dates or dinner and movies with friends; because I always kept loose change around.

Later on in life, I would find myself reading several books such as "Think and Grow Rich" by Napoleon hill, "The Way to Wealth" by Benjamin Franklin, and "The Richest Man in Babylon" by George S. Clason. All in which taught me the importance of savings and ownership. In George S. Clason's book, "The Richest Man in Babylon", I was taught to always keep 10% of all that you make. Needless to say, it has created an outlet in which I can create a large amount of wealth from a small amount of income.

A study conducted in The Wall street Journal, by Pew Research Center, showed that "The median wealth of white households is 20 times that of black households and 18 times that of Hispanic households." Household wealth is defined as the sum of assets. Which are houses, cars, stocks and mutual funds. Minus the sum of debt, which is mortgages, auto loans, the study defines. As a result, the typical black household had just $5,677 and the typical Hispanic household had $6,325 in wealth, while the typical white household had $113,149.It is now a proven fact that African Americans, are not being taught the importance of finances, when assets and liabilities are involved.

The lack of knowledge of ownership and wealth not only jeopardizes our living standards, but it affects our communities as well. In 2004, President George W. Bush, envisioned a concept where each American family would own a house and a stock portfolio. He believed our country would be more stable and prosperous. Though the vision never came true, it was actually a great idea, especially if it had been given the opportunity to trickle down into urban communities.

As read in a article by David Boaz, "People have known for a long time that individuals take better care of things they own. Homeowners take better care of their houses than renters do. That's not because renters are bad people; it's just that you're more attentive to details when you stand to profit from your houses rising value or to suffer if it deteriorates. "His article brings great truths when he states, "Just as homeownership creates responsible homeowners, widespread ownership of other assets creates responsible citizens. People who are owners feel more dignity, more pride, and more confidence. They have a stronger stake, not just in their property, but in their communities, and society."

Many people are killed and are living in poverty in many urban areas across America. There are those who actually believe people living in urban communities have poor mentalities due to living in harsh conditions and environments; but that is most certainly untrue. The crimes that are being committed are being done because of the lack of opportunity and resources. We fight for the crumbs that were left on the dinner table by the wealthy to try and survive. These actions are being committed because of the need of survival. John Kenneth Galbraith's, "The Affluent Society ", states that a society which has privately owned resources were generally clean, efficient, well- maintained improving in quality, all while public spaces (normally where minorities reside) were dirty, overcrowded, and unsafe.

We have to deprogram our minds on the idea of what true happiness and wealth is. Happiness and wealth does not consist of new shoes, leased cars or the newest cellular phone. It is the sense of being able to not only enjoy the fruits of your labor, but also own a portion of that in which you make. It always saddens me to find out the lack of interest of people who do not invest a small portion of their income, into the company's 401k plan. When given the opportunity, I try to teach and convince that it is imperative to make the investment; because even after you may decide to resign or retire. You have the opportunity to own a portion of the company that you invested your labor in.

I recommend that we all start today. Let's rise up to a world ruled by capitalism. We must make wise decisions and begin to invest and contribute to our futures. Let's begin to focus on taking pride in being *a owner*, and not a *slave*.

THE MANY STAGES
OF THE NEGRO

The development and differences in today's age of Negroes come from the migration of southern slaves after Civil war. This migration not only allowed blacks to move throughout the United States, but it also helped create opportunities for blacks to learn, and flourish in a much better environment. The migration to the north created better opportunities for blacks. These opportunities helped grant blacks the ability to obtain success, ownership and wealth; three components that was and still is a part of every Americans definition of the "American Dream".

From the first Afro American to own a Cadillac to the tenants who migrated from the south to live freely and dormant in Harlem; the image of the black man and woman has increased tremendously. The black man and woman in America have evolved at alarming speeds. Having had done so, there has not been an urgency of personal ethics to be taught and embedded into his or her mind. Our wants of status, image, and belonging has replaced ou culture, values, and moral.

My observations to the differences between different Afro Americans internalized while conversing with a Hispanic lighting director in L.A. This conversation started on set, while working with an Indian film production company for Bollywood in 2008. While working, the lighting director admitted to me that he held a certain disgust in the way western black men dressed themselves compared to those black men living on the east . He drew comparisons of how a black man from the east coast, would never wear dirty shoes for the sake of their public image in New York City. He was amazed to see how black men on the west coast presented themselves to look subpar, and how they held little concern on how anyone would view them. This immediately made me take notice to not only my own appearance, but others around me as well.

Having had the opportunity to live in both the north and south. I have had the opportunity to compare and contrast the many differences between a southern raised and northern raised Afro American. My comparisons were drawn from the senses of what we desire based around Maslow's Hierarchy of Needs. I was introduced to the hierarchy of needs through my basic introduction courses of marketing in college. Maslow's theory is a psychology theory that is categorized in 5 parts. These 5 parts include self-actualization, esteem, love/belonging, safety, and physiological. A pyramid represents the theory; the largest and most fundamental levels of needs are at the bottom, and the need for self-actualization at the top.

For each category, I was able to draw comparisons to the levels of needs and wants from a northern Afro American and southern African American. All in which of who share a large amount of the same ancestry, but manages to live completely different lifestyles. In my observation, I have come to find that this is not only a lifestyle, but an attitude and state of mind. The difference in which those who place their needs and wants above the Christian Belt are different from those below it.

Based upon Maslow's theory, Northern African American men and women most important need would be esteem. Maslow believed that there is two versions of esteem needs, "a lower one and a higher one. The lower one is the need for the respect of others, the need for status, recognition, fame, prestige, and attention. The higher one is the need for self-respect, the need for strength, competence, mastery, self-confidence, independence and freedom. The latter one ranks higher because it rests more on inner competence won through experience. Deprivation of these needs can lead to an inferiority complex, weakness and helplessness."

When you focus on the psyche of a Northern African man and woman, it is one that thrives off of public image, status, and recognition. African Americans in the north pride themselves on staying in the "know" or with the latest of whatever may be on the cutting edge. Whether it is technology, fashion, or automobiles. They also require respect and attention from all of their counter parts, two attributes in which Maslow considers to be a part of lower needs. There higher needs also come from strength and independence, which is due to their high level of perseverance and resiliency. The north is full with a lot of competition, which in returned has made the Afro American male and female very competitive. They are not only faced with competition, but survival as well. Unlike those African Americans in the south, north Afro Americans must compete with a wide range of people ranging from different cultural backgrounds.

The northern African American believes that image and status is everything within society. Success is defined by what you have obtained. Your image and status is what differentiates you while living amongst others, and for a northern African American, image and status solidifies your reputation. This making Maslow's need of self-actualization, second to a northern Afro American. Self-actualization explained by Maslow "pertains to what a person's full potential is and realizing that potential. Maslow describes this desire as the desire to become more and more of what one is, to become everything that one is capable of becoming." Often in the north, Afro American's envision their selves as being seen as a particular individual. A persona or public image that an Afro American creates based upon how they would like to be received within society. This public image protects northern African Americans from the actual truth of whom and what they are truly made of.

47

Having had also been given the opportunity to live in the south for several years. I was also granted the luxury of defining what southern African American needs are based upon Maslow's hierarchy as well. Through my own observation I found that southern Afro Americans all share the sense of Love and Belonging and Safety.

Maslow defines his Love and Belonging as a need to feel a sense of belonging and acceptance, whether it comes from a large social group, such as clubs, office culture, religious groups, professional organizations, sports teams, gangs, or small social connections (family members, intimate partners, mentors, close colleagues, confidants). Is it not factual to see that southern African Americans have larger churches, black fraternities and sororities, and families than those living in the north? I found that their idle time is spent in groups that consist of mostly family or friends that they have known for very long periods of time. This need is much greater to southern African Americans opposed to northern. They really know the importance of belonging and love in society.

Safety is another huge need for southern Afro Americans. Through family members, southern African Americans are taught the importance of assets vs. liabilities. They may have family members who own acres of land. They may also own or live in larger homes. This all showcases their needs for property, and ownership. I find that the idea of ownership and stability is far much more valued to southern Afro Americans. Whereas, northern African Americans are comfortable with renting and leasing whatever they may own.

You may say to yourself that this is all determined upon a person's individualism, but I digress. Having had met so many people with the same ideas and notions I can only view individualism as groups within the African American community. For African Americans, individualism is a requirement. Though individualism is seen as a separation from the norm in society, many people emulate and replicate what they see encounter without actually realizing it. In our culture individualism is used to classify and associate a group of people with one another. I find that individualism, lifestyle, and attitudes all help create characteristics, for blacks. Fashion labels, music, and status all play a huge role in the embodiment of a northern and southern Afro American.

My own personal experience and interaction with southern Afro Americans, is that individualism, and the need of separation from what may seen as norm in society is not much of a need. Southern African Americans are more immense with pop culture, and what may be nationally or regionally accepted opposed to accepting something because of their sense of individuality. Southern Afro American's individuality is in the choice of their vehicles, homes, and health, rather than appearance and status.

Northern Afro Americans sense of individualism is more diversified than southern African Americans. Northern African Americans have the opportunity to live amongst other cultures, which help diversify their characteristics, personality, and appearance. What is normally accepted within society is offset with the knowledge and dealings of different ethnic backgrounds. These exceptions help create a broader acceptation for northern African Americans when it involves individuality. Northern Afro Americans are more open to expressing themselves through fashion and style of dress than southern. Public image helps with presenting the idea of social status through appearance.

If and when given the opportunity to use all these notions within my ideology. I believe Afro Americans can become a much better developed class of people. Not implying that we as Afro Americans aren't, but once compared to other races. We are far less structured. This is due to the fact of disassociation and separation within our culture. Migration to other states or countries is also an attribution to the decline of our success. Once we migrated from our origin, our sense of values and ethics changed. I believe once we intertwine our core values from across all other regions. We will have the ability to live a much better lifestyle.

THE WAR FOR LIBERATION

When talking with people I always ask if I'm talking to much because I always feel as if I am. One day while conversing with my mother, we happened to begin reflecting on my younger days growing up as a child. She informed me that in elementary school, my teacher actually believed that I should be placed in special-ed because I talked so much. I was disturbed when I heard this. I couldn't understand why someone would actually believe that a child should be placed in special education just because they expressed how they feel.

I personally feel that the public school system is a place for the development of a real education. It is a institution created for the conditioning of people who will soon succumb to becoming a wage slaves. Nothing is really taught, and there isn't enough teachers, classrooms, or resources to focus attention on each individual child. I have found that Afro American children and teens are very gifted. Yet little focus is placed on the gifts and talents that these children have.

My love and concern for our development in society began in high school, when working part-time at a day care center. This soon grew into my interest in possibly working with children in my future. It was within a daycare that I seen that moral, character, and values are impetrative to teach at a early age. It was there, in which I saw that a true sense of nourishment has to be instilled in a child, in order for he or she to go about their day in the world.

Without these key components, a child will wanders into the world looking to inflict pain and hurt amongst people.

During the year of 2011, I took on a part time job as a administrative assistant with a company called Youth Consultation Services at the legendary Eastside High School, from the movie 'Lean on me'. Having had the opportunity to go back inside the school system and see the mentality of the youth actually gave me the chance to see and witness what we're up against collectively as a people. I must truly say that we are truly behind as not only a people, but also a nation. The value of education is no longer a priority, and the want and need for status is at an all time high.

The educational system is truly failing us because while working there I seen the lack of concern for those people faced with disparity. This is a nation wide issue within our community. I was truly naïve to the fact that there could be African Americans who could not to this day still read and write. All until I was there and seen the many issues that young minorities are faced with at this day of age and it is truly devastating. Never have I seen a educational institution that replicated a prison, Students being treated like inmates within a prison.

There is less attention and focus being placed on our teenagers. Therefore they turn to acts of crime or violence because of a weak and poor educational system. These systems do not give them inspiration, because the teachers are lazy and in often times are there to only collect a check. The children are going unattended, and aren't given true outlets to focus their energy every year creates a new cycle of young teenagers who choose to drop out of school. This is an ongoing issue, and being a product of a public school I now know why.

There isn't love or concern. There are no open discussions on feelings or needs. There aren't people giving back or informing these young teenagers on which roads to take. The T.V. and music are taking the places of the teacher. Most of the youth of today know very little of achievement and triumphant because they don't have a guide or image being projected to them. Their mind isn't allowed to grow and blossom. They are being conditioned in becoming complacent to receive a dollar to survive or going to jail. Either way, the system prepares them for failure.

My time spent there within the walls of Eastside High School, provided me inspiration to do what is needed to for the community and youth. Using my own image and knowledge to convince them that there is a better outcome then what they may actually think or believe. I found it important to walk through those doors everyday with a shirt and tie daily. My purpose was to evoke their mind. I made a commitment to plant a seed in the mind of those young people who seen me. So they can see and believe that it's more to what they see on a television and computer screen.

There only going to be a selected few who are going to truly grasp the importance of education while in school in the Afro American community. Education is the only true way to freedom and liberation. It's imperative for us to teach our youth, and begin leading by example. If we start and begin to nurture our children at an early age , than the possibilities of them excelling is endless. We need a better structure and platform. We have to force the public school systems to create a better method of learning, so young children and teenagers can redirect their energy into unlocking their inner potential.

IT TAKES A VILLAGE

I find it sad that once a African American earns a substantial amount of money he or she believes their next best successful thing to achieve in life is to move out of the neighborhood that helped raise them. This very thought that with being financially stable creates the opportunity in having better living standards. This decision showcases that there is a lack of education, services and products, and community involvement in our neighborhoods. It also indicates that there is a lack of appreciation for not only the community but also the environment.

While driving with a colleague, I was informed that the community in which they were raised in made them ashamed. I could only look in amazement. How can this person who once lived and was raised by this community be ashamed of where they are from? Not only was I saddened, but quit frankly I was offended. This very person has family who lives in the very same community, so it only makes me wonder are they ashamed of them as well.

Many questions rise after I hear the words of those people who consider themselves successful and resilient to the community they once called home. Questions such as, why haven't those who have become successful lent a helping hand to the people in their community after they have "made it". Why is there a sense of urgency to leave where you been raised, and then only to return to ridicule the place you once called home? Why haven't you used your knowledge and skills to help educate those in your former neighborhood?

I perfectly understand the logic of wanting more, and having the better things in life. This is America, and it makes perfect sense to obtain more, when you earn a better income. My only problem with the idea of the "American dream" is the forgotten idea of the "American nightmare". The poverty that exists, and the poor attempt to help make contribution to build a better society. The only way this can be made possible is by teaching what has been taught to those that are successful and contributing to community involvement.

How can we gravitate to something that isn't yours to call your own ? We continuously show our support in that of which is not supportive of us. There should be a mirroring image of the things in which we support. If we use, consume, or wear a product the companies and manufactures should support us. The companies who produce trash that linger in the streets in our communities should be supportive enough to create awareness programs about pollution. It is important that the companies we invest our hard owned money in is supporting their customers. If we are the people who are helping these companies obtain their wealth, it should be fair that we obtain their support.

This is a mindset that should be acquired by those within the black community, and those who have moved into suburbia. Even though you may not live in the urban community, you still have people who have to be raised there long after you move far away. The idea of feeling successful should not come from the idea of having had "made it" and accomplishment of moving out of the urban community.

My question to those who have made it is, do you now feel apart of a bigger cause? Do you feel accepted socially? Does your status equate to happiness? Finally, what satisfaction can possibly be obtained if you choose not to reach one and teach one?

A great quote is "It takes a village to raise a child." In order to do so we need more chiefs to instruct the village, because without them. There will be no direction.

THE MATRIX
(A DECLINE IN
EVOLUTION)

"We lived on farms, we lived in cities, Now we will live on the internet."- Sean Parker from the movie "Social Network"

Like the crack epidemic in the mid and late 80's, the Internet has spread like a wild fire in a forest. Not only has it become much more of a everyday need. It has become an essential in the lives of mainly every existing human being. Similar to the drugs that have brought so much turmoil to those families of drug abusers; I have come to believe the internet has in some shape or form done the same.

Recently while riding on a elevator within a place I was visiting. I began to create my very own compare and contrast. I, unlike every other person on the elevator, was the only person not clutching onto my cell phone. As I looked around in the tightly secluded elevator, I noticed every person aboard. With there heads down, and eyes glued to their small devices clutched in the palms of their hands. Never exchanging eye contact or uttering a simple good morning or how are you?

Welcome my friends, to the Matrix! The world where very few people live sociably amongst their friends, family and peers, and where your every thought can be monitored, viewed, "liked", and, or followed. Where with one click of a button. You can become friends with thousands of people across the world. The very place where the very first black president of America was helped to become elected, and a Egyptian Revolution began.

Yes, by anyone else's standards this would seem like a place where great attributions and successes are made, but much destruction has gone unnoticed by its users. Especially amongst the next generation of youth, who are being grown, groomed, and educated through a wide strand of social networks. Networks in which has helped decrease the proper use and value of literacy, and the English language within African American communities. The need to seem 'cool,' does not consist of proper grammar and it goes overlooked. Which soon, will help depreciate the way a child or teenager will write essays, resumes, and apply for jobs.

Yes, the Internet does have its perks when it comes to creating business, marketing, and building relationships. However, it still has flaws. There have been private matters being brought public, and exposure to situations that just should not be shared outside of one's home, such as the information collected by Google, and the rights to own whatever you post on face book. This being done by the user's ability to obtain free information, and given the opportunity to share and receive immediate responses to what he or she thinks.

The Internet has had the opportunity of making everyone who now uses it a reality star. It has the ability to help someone project a image they would like the general public to believe. This allows people to post pictures and create their own personal brand which I would like to call 'Brand Me.' Brand me is the way you believe people should see you, opposed to who and how you really are in society. Brand me, is simply endorsed and promoted throughout the Internet, and is highly believable. That is not until a spectator is granted the opportunity of meeting someone outside of his or her digital existence. Only then will you be given the chance to learn who a person truly is.

I remember in college learning about the, "Muted group theory", from a friend who studied social work. She went on to explain to me that it's a theory shared amongst most people living in urban communities. The theory best described by, Mark Orbe, consisted of research which believed "Dominant white European culture has created a view of African-American communication "which promotes the illusion that all African-Americans, regardless of gender, age, class, or sexual orientation, communicate in a similar manner."

With the help of the Internet the theory has grown to become factual, by my own opinion. The Internet helps individuals from different states all live on one accord, sharing the same mental wavelength. It has the ability to keep the masses mute, and restricted. This ability was not possible in the past, once we were granted free speech. Now the forms of communication for "free speech" have changed. People are scared to truly voice their opinions publicly.

Recently a young man was shot and killed by police officers down the street from where I live. He was suspected to have a weapon, in which the officers stated that he flashed and ran off. This caused the officers to shoot the man. The officer stated the shooting was justifiable due to a "face to face" altercation. The gun on the witness was found empty, and the bullet casings were found at the scene of the crime in where he fled. I don't believe someone would be given the opportunity to shoot and run in a face-to-face altercation.

Many people mourned his death. Others wanted to seek out justice. Oddly enough, most of it was entirely done through the Internet. Unlike in the past, where in such places like California and Chicago, where people would band together and cry out injustice. He was mourned momentarily with status messages, and tweets. Even disputes from the community where locals called him a thug and criminal, was shared through the state's newspaper website. Such comments complimented the cop for murdering the young man and seeing it as "One less thug on our streets". Comments like this showcase that our war on the lack of education, poverty, and society has been brought to the digital forefront. Yet, there are very few fighters on our front line, who can or will engage in this war.

It took us approximately 465 years to overcome physical slavery, only to become mentally enslaved by a digital world. All in which is considered the matrix. A place where far less action is being done, and much more talk occur. This device multiplies its speed for destruction each year, creating new social networks for the masses to take part in. Participation in which enforces illiteracy, and destruction. This is a revolving cycle that must be broken, and taken into consideration for the education of our youth.

THIS IS IT

I went to from hustler, to activist, to philanthropist. To say I didn't start from the bottom would truly be a lie. I still remember the day when my mother convinced me to go back to college after possibly deciding to work at the United States Post Office. She truly helped me escape from the plantation, and gave an offering hand in my liberation.

Like Malcolm X, I have lived several different lives in a short period of time. Through my journey in life, I have grown through education. It wasn't struggle that helped me mature and blossom. It was the opportunity to seek out the answers to my many questions. Answers in which helped define my purpose in life. I have come to learn that we all live with purpose.

Having the opportunity to travel and partake in different cultures has helped me understand that power lies in numbers. The people who live inside a community are just as important to one another as politicians are within a government. We all account for something. Traveling to Africa to visit the Pyramids of Giza, during the Egyptian Revolution, taught me the importance of people. This in return helped inspire me to create my non-profit organization, The Outreach and Uplift Foundation. It was the sight of a people working together to fight for democracy and equality, which helped me to return to create a uproar.

My mission is to truly show, that money is only an object. It is love, respect, and appreciation of life that truly helps people rise to a better lifestyle. Being selfish creates stagnation. Afro Americans can grow to become a true powerhouse through love and the empowerment of each other.

The educational system has failed, and the children are now being taught through television and music. What will happen to the people of a community without nourishment, love, and education? Destruction! What will happen to the people without a support system within their community? Dependability from the government!

It is through the power of observation, pride, and will that help in my vow to make a change and difference. I have been given the opportunity to be set free as a slave, and become a free man through education. I have been given the opportunity to teach, and advocate for those people who are lost and entrapped by a system that was created to help keep minorities dormant.

It is my passion to lift the hopes and spirits of the dreamers forced to wake up to a paradox and façade of false hopes and beliefs. This is my challenge, to any reader who believes they are selfless; to pursue any challenge and overhaul those obstacles that hold you back from becoming great.

As I once read it from a book entitled "Think and Grown Rich" by Napoleon Hill. " Life battles don't always go to the strongest or fastest man. But sooner or later, the man who wins Is the man *who thinks he can.* " These are my very thoughts. I think I can make a change and a difference, so therefore I shall. We must believe in ourselves, and no longer accept mediocrity. The shackles that once was placed on our bodies, has now been placed on our minds. It still remains a challenge to set us free all due to our constant struggles within ourselves, and our want for materialism.

We're lost because we've been misguided. Having money has become our set desire and our fight for freedom has been compensated by greed. Money cannot free us . It may create an idea of joy, but it will not liberate us as a people. Our oppression as a people is a worldwide issue, and the only way to rise above it, is to stand together.

The end of this book marks a new beginning. The memoirs that have been presented to you throughout each chapter, has given me the ability to rise above everything that I have faced. I fully acknowledge that I am a modern day slave. Though I do not work on a plantation and civil rights have been fought for the sake of my freedom. I truly do not feel much has changed. There are still people who are faced with struggle, and who have not progressed, as they should. There are still many broken homes, and uneducated people due to overcrowded public school systems. There are still people who fight for their human rights within our country. As I walk the streets, I witness that much hasn't changed from the Narrative Story told by Fredrick Douglass or The Autobiography l Malcolm X. Yet, and still there are people who still are willing to truly fight.

I will be fighting for all those who will never witness the luxury or beauty that life has to offer. I can only hope to have had an effect on you as a reader, and hope that I have enlightened you on what we face as a minority in society. My memoirs are only a small portion of what minorities are affected by.

In my efforts, I give you my promise that the Outreach and Uplift Foundation will stick to its mission statement and instill pride and courage within our youth. We will also empower, transform, and transcend the citizens of urban communities' nationwide through the usage of our involvement. There is a true need of leadership and education of social and economical awareness. The plan has been set forth, and I can only hope that you are set forth in yours. Let's Get Free!

SHORT STORIES

The following are short fictional stories that have been created to evoke thought into the readers. I hope you enjoy!

HIGH RISE FOR LOW STANDARDS

Before the start of the show, I ask my co-star how do I look? Linda, who is playing 'Mammy', says I can add just a little bit more make-up to my cheek area. I ask, how do I look now? She replies "PERFECT, It's show time!" Soon I'll be gracing the stage with my first theatrical performance. My anxiety seems to cause my heart to race one mile per minute. I look one last time in the mirror at my clothes before taking the stage.

The curtain rises, and the audience stares in amazement. Mammy begins the show with her opening line, "Welcome Y'ALL, to THE BEST MINSTREL SHOW on Earth!" There's my cue! Immediately I come out shucking and jiving, dancing and singing. Never missing a beat. I'm greeted by the laughter of the audience. Though I have very few lines, I make sure they are said with precision. "Yes Massa", "No Massa"," How may I help you Massa", "Is there "ANYTHING ELSE" I can help you with Massa." The crowd eyes are locked in on me. They are impressed with my stagnant performance. The show ends, and we all take a bow. The crowd stands and claps, and begins to exit.

We all run back stage excitingly. After congratulating one another for a performance well done. I go to the bathroom and hold my head underneath the sink, to remove my 'black face'. After thoroughly cleaning the make up away, I hold my head high to look myself in the mirror, only to be greeted with the very thing

I just washed away. I have been hiding behind the very thing that I have been performing in. The only difference between the character and myself is the intelligence I hold within my brain. I grow angry, and continue to repeat to myself that I am doing this for a bigger cause, and I should not allow my integrity to get the best of me. After convincing myself, I exit the bathroom and make my way outside.

When I open the door, I am approached by a small group of fans, which would like autographs. The father of a family approaches me, with his two small children. He says, "My name is John, and these here are my two children Billy and "Christina. They loved your performance." I smile, and thank him. He then asks me "What is your name?" I reply Jerard. He replies well Mr. Jerard, I must say . "You are the best NIGGER, I have ever seen perform in the MINSTREL SHOW!"

I stand there hurt. I'm not sure if I should smile or cry. My integrity resurfaces, and I am reminded that even though I removed the "black face" underneath the sink moments ago. I am still in character. I ask myself, "How do I respond?" While standing they're in silence. My "mind" begins to formulate my response. I am reminded once again that there is a man with a brain, and intelligence that stands before this small crowd that awaits me for autographs. I then respond, "Yes Mr. you stand correct. I am the BEST NIGGER you will EVER SEE." He looks in astonishment, and I continue on to sign his children autographs. To Billy and Christina, thank you for witnessing the future. From yours truly, "THE BEST NIGGER TO EVER DO IT, JERARD SHANNON "

IS IT THE SHOES?

A whole entire paycheck spent in a matter of 8 hours all while spending on a new sneaker release. Who's going to tell me I'm not the flyest today? I now own the new Air Jordan's, before the actual release date. With a few extra dollars left over, I figured I would buy a matching shirt, and fitted cap as well.

Morning arrived and I had showered. I then ironed my clothes precisely and began to lace my new Jordan's perfectly. I had a few errands to complete today, so on my way I went.

While out I made sure I walked slowly, so I can catch the eyes of spectators who stared at me wearing the new releases shoes. Which had cost me two hundred dollars. Hell, I better had been seen and complimented for missing two of my bill payments.

After stopping at some of the local stores within my neighborhood, reminded myself that I needed to few items from the local supermarket located downtown. So I decided to catch the next bus was let off a few stops before the retail store.

While making my way to my destination, I began to notice the feel of stares that were not similar to the ones I just was greeted with back in my neighborhood. These stares belittled me, and were unwelcoming. As I walked further I noticed the pace in several individuals walking speed, which increase. I also witnessed the sights of women clutching their purses as if I was I was a thief. I felt as if I did not belong, I began to walk faster so I could hurry and arrive at my destination.

Finally after walking a few blocks, I finally arrived. I grabbed a shopping cart and began to do my shopping. The stares and discomfort I felt began to lessen .I picked up my items after shopping down each isle frantically, and joined the express lane.

A small child then greeted me. The child tugged at my newly shirt and began to laugh. I smiled not knowing why the child was determined to pull at my shirt but I began to see each pull intensified Finally after a several tugs and laughs, the child's mother came over to apologize for her kids action. She asked the young boy why he playing with the nice gentleman. The child replied "He looks like one of the clowns I seen at the circus with you and daddy, mom". The woman looked at me shamefully, and apologized for her sons comment. She picked her son up, and walked off.

I couldn't believe my ears. A small child with no sense of style or fashion has just compared my appearance to a clown. I felt insulted, but I also grew curious. I grew curious to see what he seen I left off the shopping line, and found my way to the home section looking to try and search for a full length mirror. Finally I found one.

With great disbelief, I must say the child was right. My size 8 ½ new Jordan sneakers, looked no different than those shoes worn by a clown during his performance. My outfit, which I tried so hard to color coordinate also did me no justification. I was taken away. I could now understand why, during my travels to the retail store the stares I received made me feel so awkward. I was not adapting to my surrounding. I thought I looked well groomed, but in all honesty I looked foolish.

Here I spent two hundred dollars of my hard earned money on basketball shoes and didn't never stepped one foot on basketball court that day. I felt foolish and ashamed. To add more insult to injury, a child had told me how foolish I looked. I was instantly reminded by a quote said by Frank Lucas, a character played by Denzel Washington in the movie American Gangster while he was conversing with his brother about fashion. " The loudest dressed person in the room is the weakest person in the room."

With that immediate reminder I made a vow to never purchase a pair of highly expensive sneakers again. I chose to become financially savvy and invest into things that are more cost efficient. One of those purchases being a pair of hard bottom shoes to help make me look professional. All so I can never be seen or taken as a joke ever again!

PREPACKAGED

Great! I enter my car just to be delightfully welcomed to my check engine light. I guess everything I had planned for the day will be delayed until I find out what the problem is. I immediately drove my car to my mechanic who is located in the next town over. I explained the problem, and was told to leave the car to be worked on. My mechanic drove me back to my house, and I was left without my vehicle for the rest of the day.

The next my mechanic called me and told me the work was complete and I could pick up my car. I started my day with my daily routine and than got out my clothes for the day. My name brand clothing was neatly ironed, and my expensive cologne was then sprayed on several areas of my body. I was now prepared to get my vehicle. The weather was quite fair that day, so I decided a walk instead of using public transportation. I exited my home, and made my way up on my journey.

While on my journey I began to take notice to the architectural details of the homes in my neighborhood, and the people within my community. As I began to take notice very disturbing images and acts. On my stroll I found myself stepping over drug paraphernalia, and liquor bottles. I began to take notice to the trash along the streets, and the graffiti of gang signs on the walls. I saw abandoned buildings, and stray animals looking to find a meal. As I journeyed further I witness fiends who have fallen victim to drugs. I witnessed unattended children, who played in the streets while cars passed them by. Nearly, escaping death, if the provision of the driver was not attended.

I witnessed churches and liquor stores all within the same 5-mile radius. I couldn't help but think that this is the same way of countless neighborhoods in many African American communities throughout the United States. Why is this?

Almost near my destination, I noticed there was a bridge that separated the very town that I just left. Once crossing underneath the bridge, I found myself in a seemingly more pleasant place. A place where there was little to no trash on the streets. Where garbage cans resided on each corner, and playgrounds were present for children. I noticed children playing within the playground and not in the street. The faces were all full of joy. There were no abandoned buildings in sight, and the animals that were in attendance were on leashes, and not roaming the streets.

I began to feel sickened and ill fainted. The clothes that I bared on my skin began to bear disgust. I began to find perplexities in my very thought and actions. I began to think to myself that the clothes that I wore me "look" the par. But as I traveled, I did not "feel" the par. My materialistic possessions no longer made me feel luxurious because I did not live luxurious. This whole entire time, I thought I was living a glamorous life, because of the things that I owned and wore. But the reality of it was I was not living a glamorous life, but indulging and spending my money on a lifestyle. A lifestyle that did not equate to my reality!

I stood there shocked while in front of the playground. Astounded by what my mind had just uncovered. The lies that have I have force-fed myself. I thought about all the money I invested in trying hard to hide my shamefulness of being a poor middle class citizen. I then began to think about all of the clothing designers who may have laughed continuously, all while driving on that bridge that separated their luxurious homes and neighborhood from the countless ghettos of America. Steadily growing wealthier day by day, for a lifestyle and illusion they sell to the less fortunate; who only wish to escape the hell they are living everyday through their material possessions,

I finally got it together and made my way to the mechanic shop. I paid him, and reccived the keys to my vehicle. Before exiting, he shook my hand and said " Wow your hands are very cold". I replied "Yes, but only if you could see my heart."

AND WHERE DO MOST DREAMS END UP?

As children we are asked what would you like to be while growing up? We are told that we can be anything in the world? I still remember my grandmother asking me that very question. What do I want to be when I grow up? A question and answer she often reminds me of. My reply to that question was the president. Even after being asked that question I can still recall the members of her church, calling me the president during our Sunday worshipping service. Many years later, I still have not come to see that dream come into reality.

During one of my classroom lectures during my college years, a professor asked his students who were studying and hoping to obtain careers in the field they majored in a question. The professors question was this, "Where do dreams end up?" We all looked around waiting to see who knew the answer to this question. Still waiting without an response. The professor took it upon himself to answer his question. "The graveyard" he replied. Most people's dream end up in the graveyard, laid to rest, never to see the light of day again.

One afternoon, my grandmother asked me to take her to the convenient store to play her lottery numbers. I agreed and drove her to the store. While waiting for her return I grew angrily and impatient, and began to steer at everyone in arriving their with disgust. Minute by minute I watched people enter and exit this store with smiles upon their face. Only to be given the announcement of there lost that same night. I began to grow upset that all these people stood in a line, waiting to play numbers, placing their faith and hope and DREAMS into something so unpromising, and then it immediately it hit me. I was taken back to my college professor's question during his lecture. Where do dreams end up?

I whispered to myself that within the inner city DREAMS END

UP IN A LOTTERY MACHINE! It was not the graveyard. Hell, The very slogan for the lottery is "Where dreams come true." Day by day people invest their hard earned money and faith into numbers hoping to obtain what they have laid to rest so many years ago. Looking to be compensated for the decision that led them to give up their dreams.

I started asking myself, what made these people give up on their dreams? Why did they stop pursing their hearts? Why did they settle? Did reality consume them, and force them to give up? Does age limit us in becoming accomplished?

We are all given the opportunity to purse a dream. I find the only people who take the time to pursue these dreams are those people who make it their priority to make their dream a goal. These people are not intimidated by the idea of failure. These people are not afraid to live within a world that judge you as a HAVE or HAVE NOT.

I don't recall anyone telling me or anyone else that there was a time limit on a dream in life. We was not given a time limit on the two. However it is known that time waits for no man or woman. You must use your time wisely.

I have been to the funerals of many dreamers. These dreamers have been butchered by the hardships of reality. Dreams that are not pursued because of realities demands. People forced to no longer believe in themselves, and what they can accomplish. The persistence of making dreams a reality becomes limited because a person's ambition no longer exists. Never having the opportunity to have met him, an educated guess tells me this is why Michael Jackson created NEVERLAND RANCH.

After have found solutions to my theory my grandmother entered back into my car. She apologized for the long wait, and blamed the long line of people waiting to play the lottery. I told her it's ok for the wait. I understand that you can't put a limit on a dream, and those people only want to live out just that. THEIR DREAMS!

72

Made in the USA
Middletown, DE
07 April 2023

28075440R00045